Under the Sea

Hammerhead Sharks

Meryl Magby

PowerKiDS press.
New York

To my awesome nephew, Kenny Stappert

Published in 2013 by The Rosen Publishing Group, Inc.
29 East 21st Street, New York, NY 10010

First Edition

Editor: Jennifer Way
Book Design: Greg Tucker

Photo Credits: Cover, pp. 5, 6–7, 8, 9, 11 (bottom), 12–13, 14, 17, 20, 21, 22 Shutterstock.com; p. 4 © www.iStockphoto.com/Chris Dascher; pp. 10, 16 Gerard Soury/Oxford Scientific/Getty Images; p. 11 Jeff Rotman/The Image Bank/Getty Images; p. 15 Alexander Safonov/Flickr/Getty Images; pp. 18, 19 © Andre Seale/age fotostock.

Library of Congress Cataloging-in-Publication Data

Magby, Meryl.
 Hammerhead sharks / by Meryl Magby. — 1st ed.
   p. cm. — (Under the sea)
 Includes index.
 ISBN 978-1-4488-7398-2 (library binding) — ISBN 978-1-4488-7477-4 (pbk.) —
ISBN 978-1-4488-7551-1 (6-pack)
 1. Hammerhead sharks—Juvenile literature. I. Title.
 QL638.95.S7M34 2013
 597.3—dc23
                              2011046784

Manufactured in China

CPSIA Compliance Information: Batch #WKTS12PK: For Further Information contact Rosen Publishing, New York, New York at 1-800-237-9932

Contents

Heads Like Hammers

Sharks are some of the most dangerous animals in Earth's oceans. They are fast swimmers with sharp teeth and powerful jaws. Some sharks are at the top of the ocean's **food chain**! However, there is one family of sharks that looks very different from other sharks. The sharks in this family have wide, flat heads that look like double-sided hammers or shovels. These sharks are called hammerheads.

It is easy to see how hammerhead sharks get their name. There are nine different kinds of sharks in the hammerhead family.

This is a lemon shark, which does not belong to the hammerhead shark family. There are more than 400 different kinds of sharks in the world!

Hammerhead sharks are related to other sharks, including the great white shark, blue shark, and tiger shark. Sharks in the hammerhead family include great hammerheads, scalloped hammerheads, and smooth hammerheads.

Where Hammerheads Live

Hammerhead sharks are found in warm and tropical ocean waters all over the world. They stay mostly in the parts of the ocean near the coasts of continents and islands where the water is not as deep as in the open.

Hammerheads often live in **habitats** such as coral reefs, **lagoons**, bays, and **estuaries**. They are also found far from shore, where the water is somewhat deeper. However, they are rarely seen in the very deep water of the open ocean. Hammerhead sharks often **migrate** in the summer to find cooler waters.

Hammerhead sharks tend to live in shallower waters, like that around the coral reef shown here.

Five Kinds of Fins

Sharks, such as hammerheads, are fish. This means that they are cold-blooded and breathe underwater using gills. However, unlike most fish, sharks have skeletons that are made of **cartilage** instead of bones.

Hammerhead sharks' eyes and nostrils are at the far ends of their flat, wide heads. They have small mouths filled with rows of sharp teeth.

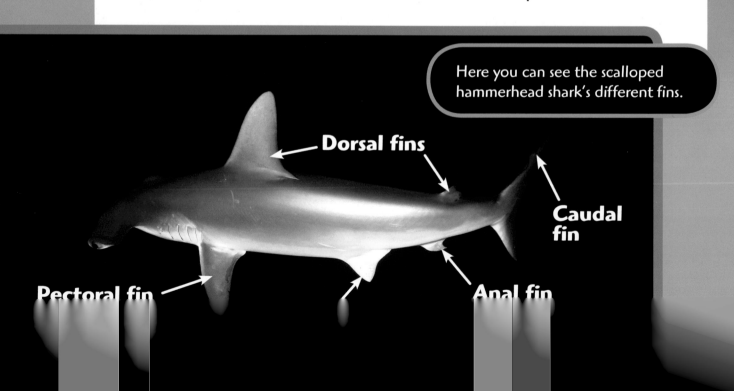

Here you can see the scalloped hammerhead shark's different fins.

Dorsal fins

Caudal fin

Pectoral fin

Anal fin

A shark's cartilage skeleton is lighter and more flexible than a skeleton made of bones would be. This helps sharks move and change direction quickly.

Hammerheads have five different kinds of fins. Their tails, called caudal fins, push them forward. The fins at the fronts of their bodies, called pectoral fins, help lift them up. The rest of the hammerheads' fins, including the dorsal fins at the tops of their bodies, keep them steady as they swim.

Helpful Heads!

There are nine different **species** of hammerhead sharks. The largest species is the great hammerhead. Adult great hammerheads can be more than 20 feet (6 m) long. The smallest species is the bonnethead. These sharks grow to be about 5 feet (1.5 m) long.

Scientists think that the shape of their heads might make it easier for hammerheads to swim or make sharp turns. They also think that hammerheads are able to

The bonnethead has a head shape that looks more like a shovel than a hammer.

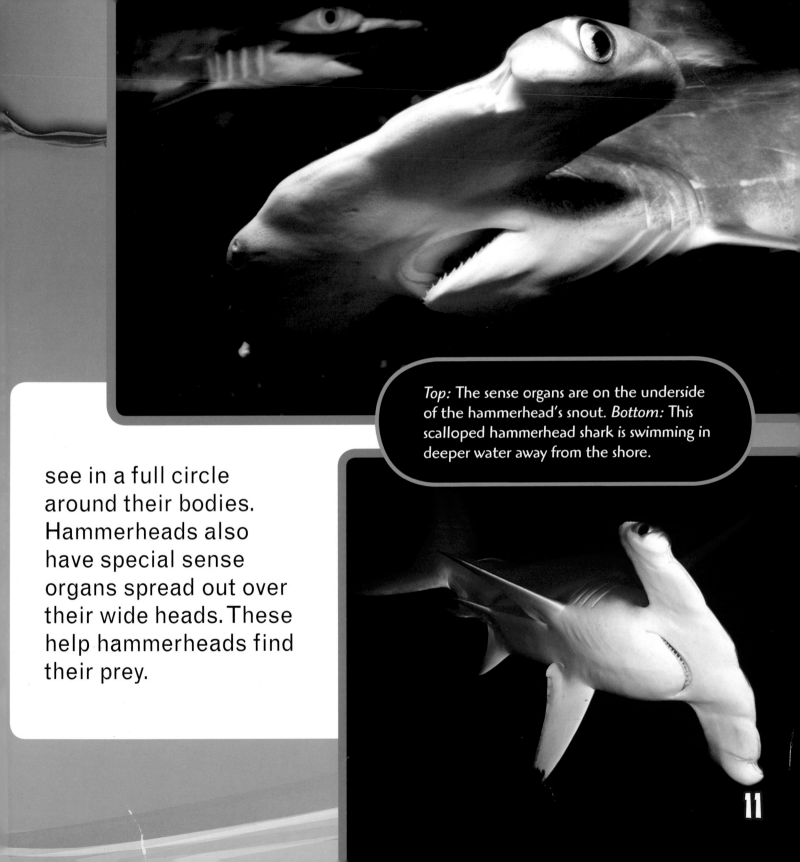

see in a full circle around their bodies. Hammerheads also have special sense organs spread out over their wide heads. These help hammerheads find their prey.

11

Hammerhead Facts

1 Hammerheads' bodies are covered in rough scales that look like small teeth.

2 Hammerheads' bodies are olive to grayish brown on top and off white on the underside.

3 Different species of hammerheads have differently shaped heads. For example, the wide head of the scalloped hammerhead is rounded with a notch in the middle. The bonnethead has a head shaped like a shovel.

4 The body of the great hammerhead shark is generally gray brown or olive green on top and off-white underneath.

5 Scientists think all hammerhead shark species living today share one **ancestor**. This prehistoric shark swam in Earth's oceans about 20 million years ago!

6 The edges of hammerhead sharks' teeth have many tiny sharp grooves, like those on a steak knife.

7 Adult great hammerheads generally weigh about 500 pounds (230 kg). However, one great hammerhead caught near Sarasota, Florida, weighed 991 pounds (450 kg)!

8 Scientists think scalloped hammerheads may use their sense organs to help them find their way when they migrate.

9 Hammerheads' favorite food may be stingrays. One scalloped hammerhead was found with 96 stingray tail barbs stuck in its mouth and jaws!

Friendly Sharks?

Many species of sharks are not social animals. This means they live alone and are not friendly toward each other. However, hammerhead sharks can be social. They often come together and form groups, or schools, of many hammerheads. Hammerheads generally travel in schools when they migrate to cooler waters during the summer months.

Scalloped hammerheads, like the one shown here, are usually not as dangerous to humans as they are to other sharks. Divers still need to be careful, though!

Hammerheads tend to migrate in schools. When they hunt for food, though, they go off by themselves.

Most species of hammerhead sharks are not dangerous to humans. This is because most hammerhead species are small and not **aggressive** toward people. However, the larger great hammerhead is a dangerous **predator**. Great hammerheads have rarely attacked humans, but swimmers should still be careful around them.

Hunting for Food

Hammerhead sharks are good hunters. They have very good vision because their eyes are so far apart. Their sense organs also tell them if prey is nearby. Some hammerheads have also been seen using their wide heads to beat their prey and hold them down. They hunt mostly at dusk.

Hammerheads feed on bony fish, **crustaceans**, squid, and sometimes even other sharks. However, their favorite food

Here is a great hammerhead catching its dinner.

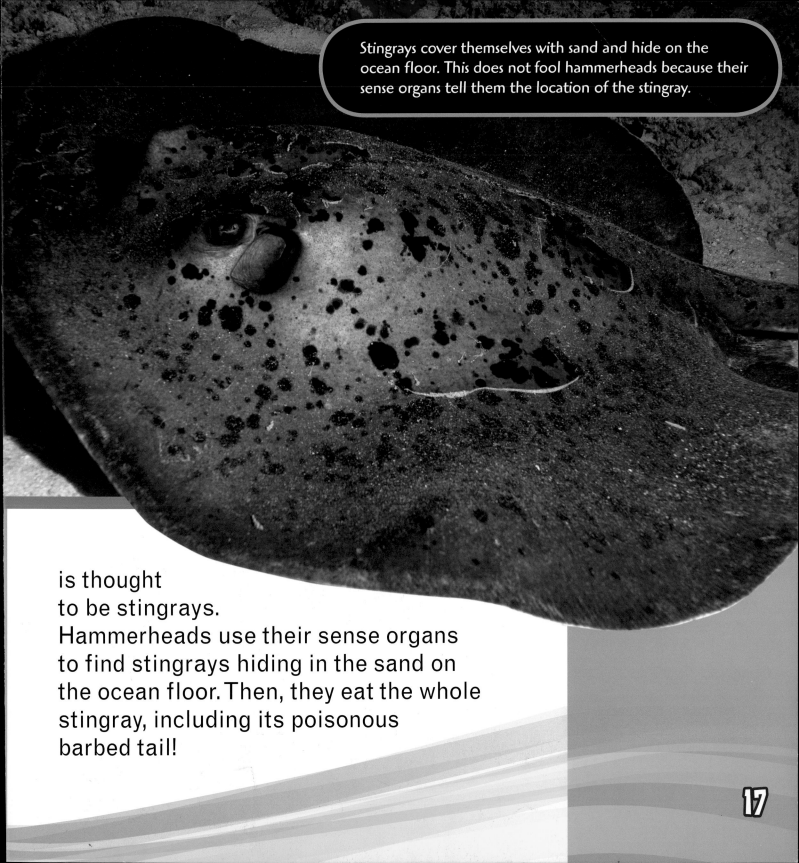

Stingrays cover themselves with sand and hide on the ocean floor. This does not fool hammerheads because their sense organs tell them the location of the stingray.

is thought
to be stingrays.
Hammerheads use their sense organs
to find stingrays hiding in the sand on
the ocean floor. Then, they eat the whole
stingray, including its poisonous
barbed tail!

Live Births

Scientists have not been able to learn a lot about how hammerheads **mate**. This is because it is thought that many shark species mate at the bottom of the ocean.

All hammerhead sharks give birth to live babies. Most other fish lay eggs. After male and

Once they are born, hammerhead shark pups are on their own. Their parents do not take care of them after birth.

Most hammerhead species produce litters of 12 to 15 pups. Great hammerheads produce larger litters, though.

female hammerheads have mated, the female gives birth about 10 to 12 months later. Shark babies are called pups. Hammerheads are born in a group of between 6 and 42 pups, called a litter. Pups are about 2 feet (61 cm) long when they are born.

Hunters of Hammerheads

Larger sharks hunt small species of hammerheads and young great hammerheads. However, adult great hammerheads have no animal predators.

Humans are hunters of hammerhead sharks, though. People fish for many species of hammerheads, such as great hammerheads and

Larger sharks, such as great white sharks, prey on small or young hammerhead sharks.

scalloped hammerheads. They sell them for their fins, oil, and skins. Hammerheads are also caught for sport. Fishermen use longlines, bottom nets, hooks and lines, and trawls to catch great hammerheads.

In the United States, scientists are afraid that large coastal fish species such as hammerheads are being overfished. This means that the total number of hammerheads is getting smaller.

Hammerheads are hunted for their fins. They are also caught by mistake by fishermen using nets to catch other fish. This is called bycatch.

Keeping Hammerheads Safe

Scientists are afraid that the number of hammerhead sharks is getting smaller. This is because too many people may be catching and killing hammerheads. In fact, the great hammerhead and the scalloped hammerhead are already **endangered**.

However, people can keep hammerhead sharks from dying out. Fishing less and keeping the oceans clean can help hammerhead numbers grow for years to come!

The scalloped hammerhead, shown here, is endangered in part because it is "finned," or killed for its fins.

Glossary

aggressive (uh-GREH-siv) Ready to fight.

ancestor (AN-ses-ter) A relative that lived long ago.

cartilage (KAHR-tuh-lij) The bendable matter from which people's noses and ears are made.

crustaceans (krus-TAY-shunz) Animals that have no backbones, have hard shells and other body parts, and live mostly in water.

endangered (in-DAYN-jerd) In danger of no longer existing.

estuaries (ES-choo-wer-eez) Areas of water where the ocean tide meets rivers.

food chain (FOOD CHAYN) A group of living things that are each other's food.

habitats (HA-buh-tats) The kinds of land where animals or plants naturally live.

lagoons (luh-GOONZ) Shallow ponds or channels near larger bodies of ≠.

mate (MAYT) To come together to make babies.

migrate (MY-grayt) To move from one place to another.

predator (PREH-duh-ter) An animal that kills other animals for food.

species (SPEE-sheez) One kind of living thing. All people are one species.

Index

Websites

Due to the changing nature of Internet links, PowerKids Press has developed an online list of websites related to the subject of this book. This site is updated regularly. Please use this link to access the list: www.powerkidslinks.com/uts/ham/